Designed by Flowerpot Press
www.FlowerpotPress.com
CHC-0909-0620
ISBN: 978-1-4867-3112-1
Made in China/Fabriqué en Chine

Copyright © 2025 Flowerpot Press,
a Division of Flowerpot Children's Press, Inc., Oakville,
ON, Canada and Kamalu LLC, Franklin, TN, U.S.A.
All rights reserved. Can you find the flowerpot?
No part of this publication may be reproduced, stored
in a retrieval system or transmitted, in any form or
by any means, electronic, mechanical, photocopying,
recording, optical scan, or otherwise, without the
prior written permission of the copyright holder.

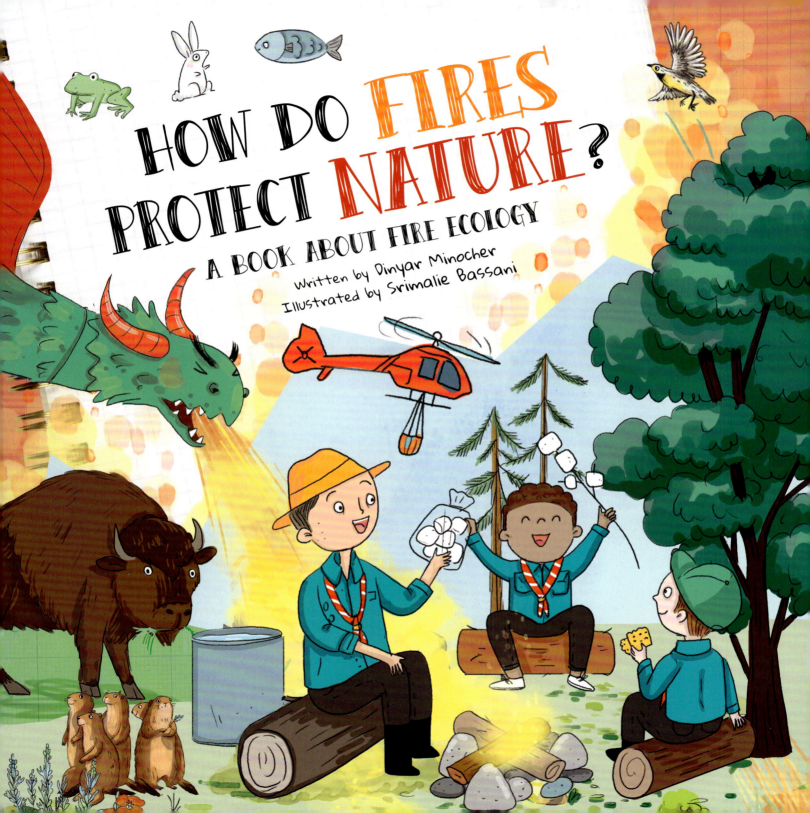

When you see an area that was recently burned, how does it make you feel? Maybe a little sad, or even scared? The blackened trees and smoky air can seem like something out of a spooky story, but actually, fires are nature's way of cleaning up and getting ready for new things to grow! Think of it as a well-needed fresh start for plants and trees. In fact, open spaces like the North American Great Plains only exist because of disturbances like grazing and browsing (animals eating plants and shrubs), climate (droughts and floods), and fire!

GREAT PLAINS

Burrowing owls are considered endangered in certain prairie lands across North America.

Fire is very good at keeping grasslands and forest floors open. Without fire, both natural and human-made, we will continue to lose grasslands and the species that call it home. Let's explore how fire is actually a friend to the plants and animals that live in the forests and prairies.

Prairie dogs are a keystone species, which means other animals rely on them!

Grasslands are one of the most endangered ecosystems on Earth and home to many endangered species.

HOW DO FIRES START?

Does a dragon sneeze after smelling too much pepper?

There are lots of different types of fires and, luckily, none of them are dragon fires! When it comes to nature, we're most often talking about wildfires and human-made fires.

For a fire to start, it needs fuel and an ignition source. The fuel can be old grasses or fallen branches, but they need to be dry enough to burn.

An ignition source is what starts the fire. Lightning is an example of a natural ignition source.

Lightning starts nearly half of the wildfires in Canada every year!

If lightning strikes a forest or prairie in the spring, when the leaves on trees and shrubs are green and plant life on the forest floor is mostly alive, it will be hard for a fire to find enough dry fuel to burn. A fire can still happen, but the intensity would be low and consumption (the amount of fuel it can burn) would be lower than the big fires we sometimes hear about.

If lightning hits the same area in late August, when the grass is yellow and cured (dry) and the forest floor is full of dry, dead plant litter, the fuels will ignite more easily and there will be more fuel to burn. This will produce a fire that can consume much bigger fuels, like trees, and it could burn up everything in that area.

In addition to wildfires, there are human-made fires. These can include accidental fires, such as campfires that weren't put out properly, electricity poles sending out sparks, or even trains making sparks along a track. Fires can also be intentional. These are called prescribed fires. These types of fires are started on purpose in a controlled way by fire experts.

Wait a minute! Sometimes people light fires on purpose and it's helpful?!

Communities, farmers, firefighters, and other trained people can plan to light low-intensity fires under very specific weather conditions that will help keep the land healthy for animals, plants, and people alike. They can do this because we acknowledge that while fire deserves our respect, it can be controlled and used as a tool under the right conditions.

Who wants smores?

Prescribed fires typically happen in the spring or the fall because weather conditions are more suitable for controlling the fire.

Think of a campfire. You wouldn't light a campfire without making a plan first. That plan would include things like setting up a safe area for your fire, having a bucket of water nearby, and making sure the conditions aren't too dry or too windy. Prescribed fires are the same way!

Fire experts prepare for a prescribed fire far in advance by creating a detailed plan and waiting for a burn window, or the time when all required conditions are met. A few things experts consider when planning a prescribed fire are ensuring there is a safe perimeter, having water and other emergency resources on site, and always having a backup plan! No one will light a single match unless the weather conditions are perfect.

HOW DO NATURAL AND PRESCRIBED FIRES CREATE HABITATS?

Do the flames put on a hard hat and use a hammer to make little animal homes?

Fires don't build the homes themselves, but they do play an important role!

Think about a deer and a ground squirrel. Do you think they have the same needs when it comes to their habitat? Of course not! Ground squirrels need wide open landscapes with short grasses to keep themselves safe from predators, while deer need areas with thick grasses or shrubby areas where they can sleep and hide. A fire can help make sure both types of habitats and more are available to the animals that need them.

As a fire moves across a landscape, it will change speed and intensity (how hot it is) depending on a lot of factors. This is important because how hot a fire burns and its residence time (how long it stays in one spot) will determine how much of the landscape is consumed by the fire. Since the fire is always changing speed and intensity, in some areas more fuel is burned and in others, less is burned. That leaves the ecosystem with a landscape that fits all sorts of habitat needs; a habitat mosaic!

A healthy forest or prairie supports a wide diversity of species, filling the many needs of the ecosystem.

Plants have specific habitat needs, too! There are so many different species of plants, trees, and shrubs, and each is looking for an area to grow and spread out. Since there's a limited amount of space, water, nutrients in the soil, and access to sunshine, some plants take up all the resources, making it hard for other plants to get the resources they need. Fire is a great way to clear out the dead and dominating species and allow for a fresh start.

If the forest floor is too thick with litter, or if a prairie has too much built-up dead grass from past growing seasons, new growth can't access the sunshine that it needs. When a fire goes through and clears the forest floor or exposes prairie soil to sunshine, plants that have been struggling to survive can push up and thrive!

HOW DO PLANTS AND ANIMALS STAY SAFE DURING FIRES?

Do they all have fire hydrants stationed outside of their burrows?

Animals don't need fire hydrants because they have been living in places with fires for a very long time and have learned to adapt. Many different animals have developed keen abilities that have allowed them to find ways to survive fires and even use them to their advantage.

Some animals, like birds and squirrels, know to quickly fly or climb away from fires to a safer place.

Other animals, like prairie dogs, badgers, and snakes, can burrow underground to protect themselves from the heat and smoke of the fire.

Some animals, like fish and amphibians, can swim in nearby rivers or lakes to escape the flames.

Sometimes animals are lost in fires, and although that may make us sad, it's important to remember that fire is just another way in which nature creates balance.

Trees, like aspens and birches, can quickly regrow new shoots from their roots after a fire. Those new roots become new trees. This process is called suckering.

Many types of grass in the grasslands and prairies, especially those native to the area, have extensive root systems that can survive a fire and quickly regrow. Just like an iceberg, most of a fire-adapted grass is underground where you can't even see it. This means most of the plant structure isn't seriously impacted by the fire.

The healthy roots are ready to start using those fresh nutrients as soon as the fire passes by. Some grasses even have seeds that wait many years for a fire and will quickly sprout afterwards, taking advantage of the new nutrients in the soil and all that newly available sunlight.

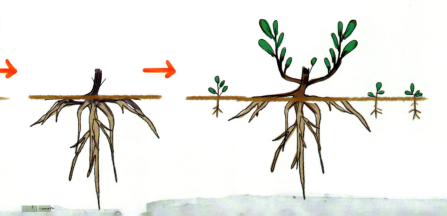

Deer, moose, and elk love fresh green plants that are often found in recently burned areas. And it doesn't stop there! The new plants can also attract insects, which in turn can be food for other animals, like birds and lizards. This creates a food web in which one animal eats another, all beginning with that initial new green growth.

Fires don't just create food for wild animals, they can also help farmers and ranchers feed their livestock.

The pastures where cows and horses graze can often get overgrown with shrubs and old plants that aren't very good for animals to eat. If the cows or horses eat too many of these old plants, they might get sick or not have enough energy to grow big and strong. Farmers and ranchers can use prescribed fires to clear the land to create space for new nutritious and tasty plants.

HOW DO PRESCRIBED FIRES HELP PREVENT MORE DESTRUCTIVE FIRES?

Do prescribed fires scare away big wildfires?

Not exactly, but they can help limit how much they destroy.

Imagine you had to clean your room. If you clean a little bit every week, it's a lot less work and takes less time. Now imagine you didn't clean your room for 5 years! There would be stuff everywhere!

Well, the same idea also applies to fire. In a controlled and safe environment, fire experts can use prescribed fires to burn away dry leaves, grass, and other things so that they don't build up over time. This helps limit the amount of litter available for the wildfire to burn and makes it easier to put out. So, although we can't always control when or where a wildfire starts, it's possible to keep it from being overly destructive.

But how do fire experts know when it's safe to burn a forest? It comes back to one of the most important parts of the burn plan: understanding the right conditions. Fires usually burn with less intensity and are easier to control in the spring and fall when there is more moisture present.

SOME OTHER USEFUL TIPS TO MAKE SURE YOUR HOUSE IS SAFE FROM WILDFIRE:

Don't stack firewood or other flammable material right next to your house.

Make sure campfires and barbecues are fully out and always use water to cool the embers.

Use fire-resistant building materials, if possible.

Don't let dry plant litter accumulate around your house or nearby buildings.

By clearing overgrown lots and old litter from around our houses, rodents and vermin have fewer places to hide. This means we're not only protecting our houses from fire but also from critters that break into our cupboards in search of food.

By now you're probably thinking like a fire scientist, and you know that not all fire is good or bad. Sometimes fire can be destructive, while other times it plays a very important role in maintaining our natural ecosystems. Fire has a place in nature, and by always being curious and learning about the natural processes around us, we can all play an important part in maintaining nature's life cycles.

SCAVENGER HUNT

By now you're probably thinking like a fire scientist, so let's put what you have learned to the test by completing this nature scavenger hunt!

What you need:
- Scavenger hunt checklist
- Clipboard (optional)
- Paper
- Pencils or markers

How it works:

1. Pick a place to explore. This can be a park, a reserve, or even your backyard.

2. Invite some friends to join you and be sure to have an adult nearby when you go out to explore.

3. See how many items you can check off the list!

SCAVENGER HUNT CHECKLIST:

1. Find three different types of leaves and compare their shapes, sizes, and colors.

Are the leaves dry or are they green?

Would these leaves fuel a wildfire? Why or why not?

2. Find an animal home (a nest, burrow, hive, etc.).

Draw a picture of what you found.

What kind of animal lives in the home you found?

How do you think this animal would protect itself from a fire?

3. Find a piece of bark from a tree.

Draw a picture of the tree and the bark.

What do you notice about the thickness or texture of the bark?

How might these characteristics help the tree survive a fire?

4. Find a water source (a pond, stream, water hose, etc.).

What are two different ways this water source could help protect against a fire?

5. Look for pine cones or seeds on the ground.

Draw a picture of the pine cones or seeds you found.

Are the pine cones open or closed?

6. Look for a natural barrier (a river, rocky area, or a field of low vegetation).

How could this natural barrier stop or slow down a fire?

Why is it important for firefighters to sometimes have places where fire can't spread easily?

AMAZING ADAPTATIONS

You now know that animals and plants have learned to adapt to wildfires in order to survive and sometimes even thrive! Here are some examples of how animals have learned to live with fires and even benefit from them.

ANTECHINUS

This little marsupial found in Australia goes into a state of energy-saving rest called torpor. By doing this, these mouse-like creatures can save their energy to find what food is left after a big wildfire.

TEMMINCK'S COURSER

This African bird lays eggs the color of ash so that they blend in with recently burned earth allowing for a better chance of survival for their offspring.

BLACK FIRE BEETLE

The black fire beetle can sense a fire miles away! The fire lets it know it is time to find a mate and lay eggs.

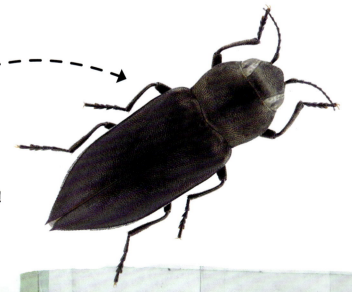

MOOSE

Moose are highly mobile and can move quickly to escape approaching fires. They often seek refuge in lakes, rivers, or marshes, where the fire cannot reach them.

BLACK-BACKED WOODPECKER

These birds actually seek out recently burned areas! They enjoy eating beetles that hide away in the charred trees.

SPOTTED OWLS

Spotted owls have been known to live on the outskirts of severely burned areas in order to hunt for small prey.

GLOSSARY

Adaptation – When plants and animals change to survive better in their environment

Browsing – When animals eat leaves, twigs, or buds from trees and bushes

Burn plan – A plan made by experts to safely manage prescribed fires

Cambium layer – The part of a tree trunk that grows new wood and bark

Climate – The average weather conditions in a place over many years

Consumption – The amount of fuel burned by a fire

Cured – When plants become dry and ready to burn in a fire

Ecology – The study of how living things interact with each other and their environment

Ecosystems – Communities of living things and their environment working together

Endangered species – Animals or plants that are at risk of disappearing forever

Firebreak – A line of cleared land, or a natural barrier, like a road or lake, that stops a fire from spreading

Fuel – Anything that can burn and provide energy for a fire

Grazing – when animals, like cows, sheep, and deer, eat grass and plants in fields or pastures

Ignition source – Something that starts a fire

Intensity – How hot and fast a fire burns

Keystone species – A plant or animal that has a big impact on its ecosystem

Prescribed fires – Fires that are intentionally set by experts to help manage forests and grasslands

Residence time – How long a fire stays in a place before moving somewhere else

Resin – A sticky substance that comes from trees and plants

Serotinous – Seeds that need fire to open and grow

Suckering – When new shoots grow from the roots of a plant

Wildfires – Unplanned fires that burn in forests, grasslands, or other natural areas